Cuddle Cocoons™

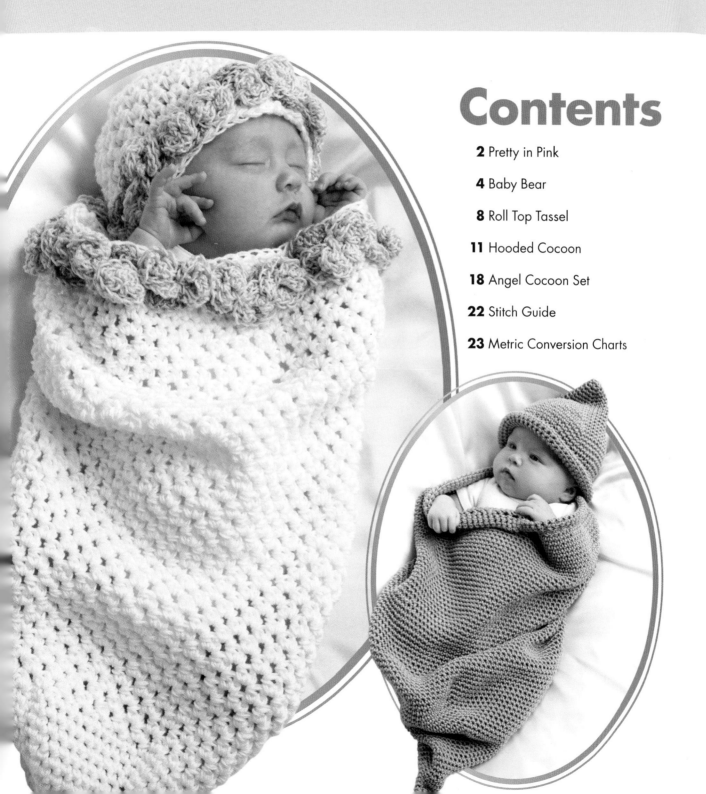

Contents

Pretty in Pink

SKILL LEVEL

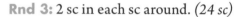

EASY

FINISHED SIZES

Instructions given fit size newborn–3 months

FINISHED GARMENT MEASUREMENTS

Cocoon: Approx 18½ inches long x
   20 inches circumference
Beanie: Approx 7½ inches long (brim down)
   x 13¼ inches circumference

MATERIALS

- Lion Brand Homespun bulky
   (chunky) weight yarn (6 oz/
   185 yds/170g per skein):
      2 skeins #392 cotton candy
      1 skein #300 Hepplewhite
- Size J/10/6mm crochet hook
   or size needed to obtain gauge
- Stitch marker

GAUGE

3 sc = 1 inch; 3 sc rows = 1 inch

PATTERN NOTES

Do not join unless otherwise stated. Use stitch
   marker or piece of contrasting color yarn to
   mark beginning of rounds.

Join rounds with slip stitch unless
   otherwise stated.

INSTRUCTIONS
COCOON

Rnd 1: With cotton candy, ch 2, 6 sc in 2nd ch
   from hook, **do not join** (see Pattern Notes).
   Mark beg of rnd (see Pattern Notes). (6 sc)

Rnd 2: 2 sc in each sc around. (12 sc)

Rnd 3: 2 sc in each sc around. (24 sc)

Rnd 4: Sc in each sc around. (24 sc)

Rnd 5: *Sc in next sc, 2 sc in next sc, rep from *
   around. (36 sc)

Rnd 6: *Sc in each of next 2 sc, 2 sc in next sc,
   rep from * around. (48 sc)

Rnd 7: *Sc in each of next 3 sc, 2 sc in next sc,
   rep from * around. (60 sc)

Rnds 8–40: [Rep rnd 4] 32 times or until
   Cocoon is approx 14 inches from beg. (60 sc)

Row 41: Now working in rows, sc in each of next
   58 sc. Leaving last 2 sc unworked, turn. (58 sc)

Rows 42: Ch 1, sc in each sc across, turn. (58 sc)

Rows 43–48: Rep row 42 6 times or until entire
   Cocoon measures approx 17½ inches from beg.
   Do not fasten off.

NECK TRIM

Rnd 1: Now working in rnds, ch 1, 2 sc in same
   st as beg ch-1 (corner), sc in each st across to
   last st, 2 sc in last st (corner), working in ends
   of rows, sc in end of each row across to rnd
   40, sc in 2 sk sts on rnd 40, working in ends of
   rows, sc in end of each row across to beg of row
   48, **join** (see Pattern Notes) in first sc. Fasten off
   cotton candy.

Rnds 2 & 3: Join Hepplewhite in first sc of
   corner, ch 1, 2 sc in same st as beg ch-1 (corner)
   and in each st around to rem corner, 2 sc in first
   sc of corner (corner), sc in each rem sc around
   to first corner, join in first sc. At end of rnd 3,
   fasten off and weave in ends.

BEANIE

Row 1: With cotton candy, ch 15, sc in 2nd ch from hook and in each rem ch across, turn. *(14 sc)*

Rows 2–40: Ch 1, sc in each sc across, turn. *(14 sc)*

Row 41 (joining row): Holding rows 1 and 40 tog, working through both thicknesses, ch 1, sc in each sc across. Leaving 6-inch tail, fasten off. Weave tail through ends of rows. Pull tight to close. Weave in ends.

BRIM

Rnd 1: Join Hepplewhite in opposite end of row 41, working in ends of rows, sc in end of each row around, **join** *(see Pattern Notes)* in first st, turn. *(40 sc)*

Rnds 2–5: Sc in same st as joining and in each rem st around, join in first st. At end of rnd 5, fasten off and weave in ends. ∎

Baby Bear

SKILL LEVEL
EASY

FINISHED SIZES
Instructions given fit size newborn–3 months

FINISHED GARMENT MEASUREMENTS
Cocoon: Approx 18 inches long x 18 inches circumference
Beanie: Approx 5 inches long x 12 inches circumference

MATERIALS
- Caron Simply Soft medium (worsted) weight yarn (6 oz/ 315 yds/170g per skein):
  2 skeins #9750 chocolate
  1 skein # 9710 country blue
- Size H/8/5mm crochet hook or size needed to obtain gauge
- Stitch marker

GAUGE
4 sc = 1 inch; 4 sc rows = 1 inch

PATTERN NOTES
Do not join unless otherwise stated. Use stitch marker or piece of contrasting color yarn to mark beginning of rows or rounds.

Chain-3 counts as first double crochet unless otherwise stated.

Join rounds with slip stitch unless otherwise stated.

INSTRUCTIONS
COCOON
Rnd 1: With chocolate, ch 2, 6 sc in 2nd ch from hook. **Do not join** *(see Pattern Notes)*. **Mark beg of rnd** *(see Pattern Notes)*. *(6 sc)*

Rnd 2: 2 sc in each sc around. *(12 sc)*

Rnd 3: 2 sc in each sc around. *(24 sc)*

Rnd 4: Sc in each sc around. *(24 sc)*

Rnd 5: 2 sc in each sc around. *(48 sc)*

Rnd 6: Sc in each sc around. *(48 sc)*

Rnd 7: *Sc in each of next 3 sc, 2 sc in next sc, rep from * around. *(60 sc)*

Rnd 8: *Sc in each of next 4 sc, 2 sc in next sc, rep from * around. *(72 sc)*

Rnd 9: Sc in each sc around. *(72 sc)*

Rnd 10: *Sc in next sc, dc in next sc, rep from * around, **join** *(see Pattern Notes)* in first st, turn. *(72 sts)*

Rnd 11: **Ch 3** *(see Pattern Notes)*, sc in next dc, *dc in next sc, sc in next dc, rep from * around, join in top of beg ch-3, turn. *(72 sts)*

Rnd 12: Ch 1, sc in same st as beg ch-1, dc in next sc, *sc in next dc, dc in next sc, rep from * around, join in first sc, turn. *(72 sts)*

Rnds 13–44: [Rep rnds 11 and 12 alternately] 16 times or until Cocoon measures 14 inches from beg. *(72 sts)*

Row 45: Now working in rows, ch 3, sc in same st as joining, dc in next sc, *sc in next dc, dc in next sc, rep from * across to last 10 sts, leaving rem 10 sts unworked, turn. *(62 sts)*

Row 46: Ch 1, *sc in next dc, dc in next sc, rep from * across, turn. *(62 sts)*

Rows 47–50: Rep row 46. At end of row 49, **do not fasten off or turn**. *(62 sts)*

NECK EDGING

Rnd 1: Now working in rnds, ch 1, sc in each end of row and in each st around entire neck opening, join in first sc. Fasten off. *(84 sc)*

Rnd 2: Join country blue in any sc, ch 1, sc in each sc around, join in first sc.

Rnd 3: Ch 1, sc in each sc around, join in first sc. Fasten off and weave in ends *(84 sc)*

BELLY (OPTIONAL)

Rnd 1: With country blue, ch 14, 2 sc in 2nd ch from hook, sc in each of next 11 chs, 3 sc in last ch, working on opposite side of beg ch, sc in each of next 11 chs, sc in same ch as first 2 sc, **join** *(see Pattern Notes)* in first sc. *(28 sc)*

Rnd 2: **Ch 3** *(see Pattern Notes)*, dc in same st as beg ch-3, 2 dc in next sc, dc in each of next 11 sc, 2 dc in each of next 3 sc, dc in each of next 11 sc, 2 dc in last sc, join in first sc. *(34 dc)*

Rnd 3: Ch 3, 2 dc in next dc, dc in next dc, 2 dc in next dc, dc in each of next 12 dc, [2 dc in next dc, dc in next dc] twice, dc in each of next 11 dc, 2 dc in last dc, join in first dc. *(40 dc)*

Rnd 4: Ch 3, dc in next dc, 2 dc in next dc, dc in each of next 2 dc, 2 dc in next dc, dc in each of next 13 dc, [2 dc in next dc, dc in each of next 2 dc] twice, dc in each of next 10 dc, 2 dc in next dc, dc in last dc, join in first dc. *(46 dc)*

Rnd 5: Ch 3, dc in each of next 2 dc, 2 dc in next dc, dc in each of next 3 dc, 2 dc in next dc, dc in each of next 15 dc, [2 dc in next dc, dc in each of next 3 dc] twice, dc in each of next 10 dc, 2 dc in last dc, join in first sc. (*52 dc*)

Rnd 6: Ch 3, dc in each of next 3 dc, 2 dc in next dc, dc in each of next 4 dc, 2 dc in next dc, dc in each of next 16 dc, [2 dc in next dc, dc in each of next 4 dc] twice, dc in each of next 10 dc, 2 dc in last dc, join in first sc. (*58 dc*)

Rnd 7: Ch 3, dc in each of next 4 dc, 2 dc in next dc, dc in each of next 5 dc, 2 dc in next dc, dc in each of next 17 dc, [2 dc in next dc, dc in each of next 5 dc] twice, dc in each of next 10 dc, 2 dc in last dc, join in first sc. Fasten off country blue. (*64 dc*)

Rnd 8: Join chocolate in same st as joining, ch 3, sc in same st as beg ch-3, (sl st, ch 1) in each dc around, join in first sc. Leaving 18-inch tail, fasten off. Using tail, sew Belly to front of Cocoon.

BEANIE
Rnd 1: With chocolate, ch 2, 12 sc in 2nd ch from hook, **join** (*see Pattern Notes*) in first sc. (*12 sc*)

Rnd 2: Ch 1, 2 sc in same st as beg ch-1, 2 sc in each rem sc around, join in first sc. (*24 sc*)

Rnd 3: Ch 1, sc in same st as beg ch-1, 2 sc in next sc, *sc in next sc, 2 sc in next sc, rep from * around, join in first sc. (*36 sc*)

Rnd 4: Ch 1, sc in same st as beg ch-1, sc in next sc, 2 sc in next sc, *sc in each of next 2 sc, 2 sc in next sc, rep from * around, join in first sc. (*48 sc*)

Rnd 5: Ch 1, sc in same st as beg ch-1, dc in next sc, *sc in next sc, dc in next sc, rep from * around, join in first sc, **turn**. (*48 sts*)

Rnd 6: Ch 3 (*see Pattern Notes*), sc in next dc, *dc in next sc, sc in next dc, rep from * around, join in first sc, turn. (*48 sts*)

Rnd 7: Ch 1, sc in same st as beg ch-1, dc in next sc, *sc in next dc, dc in next sc, rep from * around, join in first sc, turn. (*48 sts*)

Rnds 8–11: [Rep rnds 6 and 7 alternately] twice. (*48 sts*)

Rnd 12: Rep rnd 6.

Rnd 13: Ch 1, sc in same st as beg ch-1, sc in each of next 2 sts, **sc dec** (*see Stitch Guide*) in next 2 sts, sc in each of next 3 sts, rep from * around, join in first sc, turn. Fasten off. (*39 sc*)

Rnd 14: Join country blue in first st of rnd 13, ch 1, sc in same st as beg ch-1, sc in each sc around, join in first sc, turn.

Rnds 15 & 16: Ch 1, sc in same st as beg ch-1, sc in each sc around, join in first sc, turn. Fasten off at end of last rnd. (*39 sc*)

Weave in ends.

BEAR EAR
MAKE 2.
INSIDE
Rnd 1: With country blue, ch 2, 6 sc in 2nd ch from hook, join in first sc. (*6 sc*)

Rnd 2: Ch 1, sc in same st as beg ch-1, 2 sc in each sc around, join in first sc. Fasten off. (*12 sc*)

OUTSIDE
Rnd 1: With chocolate, ch 2, 6 sc in 2nd ch from hook, join in first sc. (*6 sc*)

Rnd 2: Ch 1, sc in same st as beg ch-1, 2 sc in each sc around, join in first sc, turn. (*12 sc*)

Rnd 3: With WS facing, place 1 Inside in front of 1 Outside, working through both thicknesses, 2 sc in each sc around, join in first sc.

Rnd 4: Ch 1, (sl st, ch 1) in each sc around, join in first sc. Leaving 12-inch tail, fasten off.

ASSEMBLY
Using 12-inch tail, sew each Ear to top of Beanie.

Weave in ends. ∎

Roll Top Tassel

SKILL LEVEL

EASY

FINISHED SIZES

Instructions given fit size newborn–3 months

FINISHED GARMENT MEASUREMENTS

Cocoon: Approx 21½ inches long x
25 inches circumference
Beanie: Approx 7½ inches long (brim down) x
15 inches circumference

MATERIALS

- Omega Sinfonia light (light worsted) weight yarn (3½ oz/ 232 yards/100g per skein): 4 skeins color #816 teal
- Size F/5/3.75mm crochet hook or size needed to obtain gauge
- Stitch marker

GAUGE

4 sc = 1 inch; 4 sc rows = 1 inch

PATTERN NOTES

Do not join unless otherwise stated.

Mark rounds with a stitch marker.

INSTRUCTIONS
COCOON

Rnd 1: Ch 2, 6 sc in 2nd ch from hook. **Do not join** *(see Pattern Notes)*. **Place marker** *(see Pattern Notes)* at end of rnds. *(6 sc)*

Rnd 2: *Sc in next sc, 2 sc in next sc, rep from * twice. *(9 sc)*

Rnd 3: *Sc in each of next 2 sc, 2 sc in next sc, rep from * twice. *(12 sc)*

Rnd 4: *Sc in each of next 3 sc, 2 sc in next sc, rep from * twice. *(15 sc)*

Rnd 5: *Sc in each of next 4 sc, 2 sc in next sc, rep from * twice. *(18 sc)*

Rnd 6: *Sc in each of next 5 sc, 2 sc in next sc, rep from * twice. *(21 sc)*

Rnd 7: *Sc in each of next 6 sc, 2 sc in next sc, rep from * twice. *(24 sc)*

Rnd 8: *Sc in each of next 7 sc, 2 sc in next sc, rep from * twice. *(27 sc)*

Rnd 9: *Sc in each of next 8 sc, 2 sc in next sc, rep from * twice. *(30 sc)*

Rnd 10: *Sc in each of next 9 sc, 2 sc in next sc, rep from * twice. *(33 sc)*

Rnd 11: *Sc in each of next 10 sc, 2 sc in next sc, rep from * twice. *(36 sc)*

Rnd 12: *Sc in each of next 11 sc, 2 sc in next sc, rep from * twice. *(39 sc)*

Rnd 13: *Sc in each of next 12 sc, 2 sc in next sc, rep from * twice. *(42 sc)*

Rnd 14: *Sc in each of next 13 sc, 2 sc in next sc, rep from * twice. *(45 sc)*

Rnd 15: *Sc in each of next 14 sc, 2 sc in next sc, rep from * twice. *(48 sc)*

Rnd 16: *Sc in each of next 15 sc, 2 sc in next sc, rep from * twice. *(51 sc)*

Rnd 17: *Sc in each of next 16 sc, 2 sc in next sc, rep from * twice. *(54 sc)*

Rnd 18: *Sc in each of next 17 sc, 2 sc in next sc, rep from * twice. *(57 sc)*

Rnd 19: *Sc in each of next 18 sc, 2 sc in next sc, rep from * twice. *(60 sc)*

Rnd 20: *Sc in each of next 19 sc, 2 sc in next sc, rep from * twice. *(63 sc)*

Rnd 21: *Sc in each of next 20 sc, 2 sc in next sc, rep from * twice. *(66 sc)*

Rnd 22: *Sc in each of next 21 sc, 2 sc in next sc, rep from * twice. *(69 sc)*

Rnd 23: *Sc in each of next 22 sc, 2 sc in next sc, rep from * twice. *(72 sc)*

Rnd 24: *Sc in each of next 23 sc, 2 sc in next sc, rep from * twice. *(75 sc)*

Rnd 25: *Sc in each of next 24 sc, 2 sc in next sc, rep from * twice. *(78 sc)*

Rnd 26: *Sc in each of next 25 sc, 2 sc in next sc, rep from * twice. *(81 sc)*

Rnd 27: *Sc in each of next 26 sc, 2 sc in next sc, rep from * twice. *(84 sc)*

Rnd 28: *Sc in each of next 27 sc, 2 sc in next sc, rep from * twice. *(87 sc)*

Rnd 29: *Sc in each of next 28 sc, 2 sc in next sc, rep from * twice. *(90 sc)*

Rnd 30: *Sc in each of next 29 sc, 2 sc in next sc, rep from * twice. *(93 sc)*

Rnd 31: *Sc in each of next 30 sc, 2 sc in next sc, rep from * twice. *(96 sc)*

Rnd 32: *Sc in each of next 31 sc, 2 sc in next sc, rep from * twice. *(99 sc)*

Rnd 33: 2 sc in next sc, sc in each sc around. *(100 sc)*

Rnd 34: Sc in each sc around.

Rnds 35–86: [Rep rnd 34] 52 times or until Cocoon measures approx 20 inches from beg. *(100 sc)*

Rnd 87: ***Sc dec** (see Stitch Guide) in next 2 sts, rep from * around. *(50 sc)*

Rnd 88: *2 sc in next sc, sc in next sc, rep from * around. *(75 sc)*

Rnds 89–93: Sc in each sc around. Fasten off at end of last rnd. *(75 sc)*

FINISHING
Weave in ends. Roll neck down.

TASSEL
Cut 20 strands, each approx 12 inches long. Lay strands flat and adjust so that they are equal. Cut (2) 6-inch strands of yarn. Tie one strand around middle of 12-inch strands. Fold tied strands in half. Wrap rem 6-inch strand around folded strands several times, approx 1 inch down from fold. Tie ends of strand in knot and let ends hang with Tassel strand ends. Trim ends evenly.

BEANIE
Rnds 1–19: Rep rnds 1–19 of Cocoon. *(60 sc)*

Rnds 20–24: Sc in each sc around. *(60 sc)*

Rnd 25: *Sc in each of next 3 sc, **sc dec** (see Stitch Guide) in next 2 sc, rep from * around. *(48 sc)*

Rnd 26: Sc in each sc around. *(48 sc)*

Rnd 27: *Sc in each of next 3 sc, 2 sc in next sc, rep from * around. *(60 sc)*

Rnds 28–34: Sc in each sc around. At end of last rnd, fasten off. *(60 sc)*

FINISHING
Weave in ends. Roll brim up. ∎

Hooded Cocoon

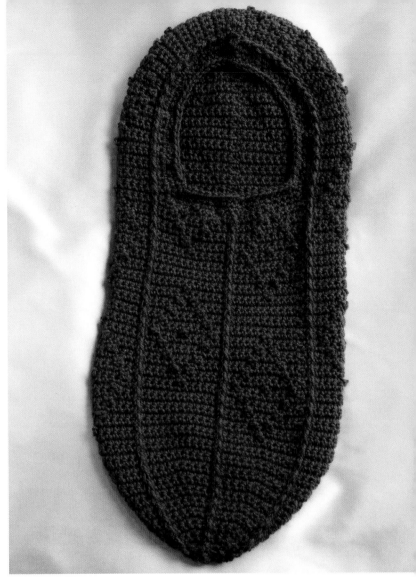

FINISHED SIZES
Instructions given fit size newborn–3 months

FINISHED GARMENT MEASUREMENTS
Approx 24 inches long x 18 inches circumference

MATERIALS
- Premier Yarns Big Ball medium (worsted) weight yarn (16 oz/ 1093 yds/454g per ball): 1 ball #29-121 coffee
- Sizes H/8/5mm and I/9/5.5mm crochet hooks or size needed to obtain gauge

GAUGE
With size I hook: 4 sc = 1 inch; 5 sc rows = 1 inch

PATTERN NOTE
Join rounds with slip stitch unless otherwise stated.

SPECIAL STITCH
Berry stitch (berry st): Insert hook in next st, yo, pull up lp, using first lp only, ch 3, yo, pull through 2 lps on hook. Push completed st to RS of work.

INSTRUCTIONS
COCOON
Rnd 1: With size I hook, ch 2, 6 sc in 2nd ch from hook, **join** (see Pattern Note) in first st. (6 sc)

Rnd 2 (RS): Ch 1, (sc, dc) in same st as beg ch-1, (sc, dc) in each sc around, join in first st, **turn.** (12 sts)

Rnd 3 (WS): Ch 1, sc in same st as beg ch-1 and in each rem st around, join in first st, turn. (12 sc)

Rnd 4: Ch 1, 3 sc in same st as beg ch-1, **fpdc** (see Stitch Guide) around next dc 2 rnds below, *sc in each of next 3 sc, fpdc around next dc 2 rnds below, rep from * 4 times, join in first st, turn. (18 sc, 6 fpdc)

Rnd 5: Rep rnd 3. (24 sc)

Rnd 6: Ch 1, sc in same st as beg ch-1, 2 sc in next sc, sc in next sc, fpdc around next fpdc, *sc in next sc, 2 sc in next sc, sc in next sc, fpdc around next fpdc, rep from * 4 times, join in first st, turn. (24 sc, 6 fpdc)

Rnd 7: Rep rnd 3. (30 sc)

Rnd 8: Ch 1, sc in same st as beg ch-1, 2 sc in next sc, sc in each of next 2 sc, fpdc around next fpdc, *sc in next sc, 2 sc in next sc, sc in each of next 2 sc, fpdc around next fpdc, rep from * 4 times, join in first st, turn. (30 sc, 6 fpdc)

Rnd 9: Rep rnd 3. *(36 sc)*

Rnd 10: Ch 1, sc in same st as beg ch-1, sc in next sc, 2 sc in next sc, sc in each of next 2 sc, fpdc around next fpdc, *sc in each of next 2 sc, 2 sc in next sc, sc in each of next 2 sc, fpdc around next fpdc, rep from * 4 times, join in first st, turn. *(36 sc, 6 fpdc)*

Rnd 11: Rep rnd 3. *(42 sc)*

Rnd 12: Ch 1, sc in same st as beg ch-1, sc in next sc, 2 sc in next sc, sc in each of next 3 sc, fpdc around next fpdc, *sc in each of next 2 sc, 2 sc in next sc, sc in each of next 3 sc, fpdc around next fpdc, rep from * 4 times, join in first st, turn. *(42 sc, 6 fpdc)*

Rnd 13: Rep rnd 3. *(48 sc)*

Rnd 14: Ch 1, sc in same st as beg ch-1, sc in each of next 2 sc, 2 sc in next sc, sc in each of next 3 sc, fpdc around next fpdc, *sc in each of next 3 sc, 2 sc in next sc, sc in each of next 3 sc, fpdc around next fpdc, rep from * 4 times, join in first st, turn. *(48 sc, 6 fpdc)*

Rnd 15: Rep rnd 3. *(54 sc)*

Rnd 16: Ch 1, sc in same st as beg ch-1, sc in each of next 2 sc, 2 sc in next sc, sc in each of next 4 sc, fpdc around next fpdc, *sc in each of next 3 sc, 2 sc in next sc, sc in each of next 4 sc, fpdc around next fpdc, rep from * 4 times, join in first st, turn. *(54 sc, 6 fpdc)*

Rnd 17: Rep rnd 3. *(60 sc)*

Rnd 18: Ch 1, sc in same st as beg ch-1, sc in each of next 3 sc, 2 sc in next sc, sc in each of next 4 sc, fpdc around next fpdc, *sc in each of next 4 sc, 2 sc in next sc, sc in each of next 4 sc, fpdc around next fpdc, rep from * 4 times, join in first st, turn. *(60 sc, 6 fpdc)*

Rnd 19: Rep rnd 3. *(66 sc)*

Rnd 20: Ch 1, sc in same st as beg ch-1, sc in each of next 3 sc, 2 sc in next sc, sc in each of next 5 sc, fpdc around next fpdc, *sc in each of next 4 sc, 2 sc in next sc, sc in each of next 5 sc, fpdc around next fpdc, rep from * 4 times, join in first st, turn. *(66 sc, 6 fpdc)*

Rnd 21: Rep rnd 3. *(72 sc)*

Rnd 22: Change to H hook, ch 1, sc in same st as beg ch-1, sc in each of next 4 sc, **berry st** *(see Special Stitch)* in next sc, sc in each of next 5 sc, fpdc around next fpdc, sc in each of next 11 sc, fpdc around next fpdc, *sc in each of next 5 sc, berry st in next sc, sc in each of next 5 sc, fpdc around next fpdc, sc in each of next 11 sc, fpdc around next fpdc, rep from * once, join in first st, turn. *(72 sts)*

Rnd 23: Rep rnd 3. *(72 sc)*

Rnd 24: Ch 1, sc in same st as beg ch-1, sc in each of next 3 sc, berry st in next sc, sc in next sc, berry st in next sc, sc in each of next 4 sc, fpdc around next fpdc, sc in each of next 11 sc, fpdc around next fpdc, *sc in each of next 4 sc, berry st in next sc, sc in next sc, berry st in next sc, sc in each of next 4 sc, fpdc around next fpdc, sc in each of next 11 sc, fpdc around next fpdc, rep from * once, join in first st, turn. *(72 sts)*

Rnd 25: Rep rnd 3. *(72 sc)*

Rnd 26: Ch 1, sc in same st as beg ch-1, sc in each of next 2 sc, berry st in next sc, sc in each of next 3 sc, berry st in next sc, sc in each of next 3 sc, fpdc around next fpdc, sc in each of next 11 sc, fpdc around next fpdc, *sc in each of next 3 sc, berry st in next sc, sc in each of next 3 sc, berry st in next sc, sc in each of next 3 sc, fpdc around next fpdc, sc in each of next 11 sc, fpdc around next fpdc, rep from * once, join in first st, turn. *(72 sts)*

Rnd 27: Rep rnd 3. *(72 sc)*

Rnd 28: Ch 1, sc in same st as beg ch-1, sc in next sc, berry st in next sc, sc in each of next 5 sc, berry st in next sc, sc in each of next 2 sc, fpdc around next fpdc, sc in each of next 11 sc, fpdc around next fpdc, *sc in each of next 2 sc, berry st in next sc, sc in each of next 5 sc, berry st in next sc, sc in each of next 2 sc, fpdc around next fpdc, sc in each of next 11 sc, fpdc around next fpdc, rep from * once, join in first st, turn. *(72 sts)*

Rnd 29: Rep rnd 3. *(72 sc)*

Rnd 30: Ch 1, sc in same st as beg ch-1, berry st in next sc, sc in each of next 3 sc, berry st in next sc, sc in each of next 3 sc, berry st in next sc, sc in next sc, fpdc around next fpdc, sc in each of next 5 sc, berry st in next sc, sc in each of next 5 sc, fpdc around next fpdc, *sc in next sc, berry st in next sc, sc in each of next 3 sc, berry st in next sc, sc in each of next 3 sc, berry st in next sc, sc in next sc, fpdc around next fpdc, sc in each of next 5 sc, berry st in next sc, sc in each of next 5 sc, fpdc around next fpdc, rep from * once, join in first st, turn. *(72 sts)*

Rnd 31: Rep rnd 3. *(72 sc)*

Rnd 32: Ch 1, sc in same st as beg ch-1, sc in next sc, berry st in next sc, sc in each of next 5 sc, berry st in next sc, sc in each of next 2 sc, fpdc around next fpdc, sc in each of next 4 sc, berry st in next sc, sc in next sc, berry st in next sc, sc in each of next 4 sc, fpdc around next fpdc, *sc in each of next 2 sc, berry st in next sc, sc in each of next 5 sc, berry st in next sc, sc in each of next 2 sc, fpdc around next fpdc, sc in each of next 4 sc, berry st in next sc, sc in next sc, berry st in next sc, sc in each of next 4 sc, fpdc around next fpdc, rep from * once, join in first st, turn. *(72 sts)*

Rnd 33: Rep rnd 3. *(72 sc)*

Rnd 34: Ch 1, sc in same st as beg ch-1, sc in each of next 2 sc, berry st in next sc, sc in each of next 3 sc, berry st in next sc, sc in each of next 3 sc, fpdc around next fpdc, *sc in each of next 3 sc, berry st in next sc, sc in each of next 3 sc, berry st in next sc, sc in each of next 3 sc, fpdc around next fpdc, rep from * 4 times, join in first st, turn. *(72 sts)*

Rnd 35: Rep rnd 3. *(72 sc)*

Rnd 36: Ch 1, sc in same st as beg ch-1, sc in each of next 3 sc, berry st in next sc, sc in next sc, berry st in next sc, sc in each of next 4 sc, fpdc around next fpdc, sc in each of next 2 sc, berry st in next sc, sc in each of next 5 sc, berry st in next sc, sc in each of next 2 sc, fpdc around next fpdc, *sc in each of next 4 sc, berry st in next sc, sc in next sc, berry st in next sc, sc in

each of next 4 sc, fpdc around next fpdc, sc in each of next 2 sc, berry st in next sc, sc in each of next 5 sc, berry st in next sc, sc in each of next 2 sc, fpdc around next fpdc, rep from * once, join in first st, turn. *(72 sts)*

Rnd 37: Rep rnd 3. *(72 sc)*

Rnd 38: Ch 1, sc in same st as beg ch-1, sc in each of next 4 sc, berry st in next sc, sc in each of next 5 sc, fpdc around next fpdc, sc in next sc, berry st in next sc, sc in each of next 3 sc, berry st in next sc, sc in each of next 3 sc, berry st in next sc, sc in next sc, fpdc around next fpdc, *sc in each of next 5 sc, berry st in next sc, sc in each of next 5 sc, fpdc around next fpdc, sc in next sc, berry st in next sc, sc in each of next 3 sc, berry st in next sc, sc in each of next 3 sc, berry st in next sc, sc in next sc, fpdc around next fpdc, rep from * once, join in first st, turn. *(72 sts)*

Rnd 39: Rep rnd 3. *(72 sc)*

Rnd 40: Ch 1, sc in same st as beg ch-1, sc in each of next 10 sc, fpdc around next fpdc, sc in each of next 2 sc, berry st in next sc, sc in each of next 5 sc, berry st in next sc, sc in each of next 2 sc, fpdc around next fpdc, *sc in each of next 11 sc, fpdc around next fpdc, sc in each of next 2 sc, berry st in next sc, sc in each of next 5 sc, berry st in next sc, sc in each of next 2 sc, fpdc around next fpdc, rep from * once, join in first st, turn. *(72 sts)*

Rnd 41: Rep rnd 3. *(72 sc)*

Rnd 42: Ch 1, sc in same st as beg ch-1, sc in each of next 10 sc, fpdc around next fpdc, sc in each of next 3 sc, berry st in next sc, sc in each of next 3 sc, berry st in next sc, sc in each of next 3 sc, fpdc around next fpdc, *sc in each of next 11 sc, fpdc around next fpdc, sc in each of next 3 sc, berry st in next sc, sc in each of next 3 sc, berry st in next sc, sc in each of next 3 sc, fpdc around next fpdc, rep from * once, join in first st, turn. *(72 sts)*

Rnd 43: Rep rnd 3. *(72 sc)*

Rnd 44: Ch 1, sc in same st as beg ch-1, sc in each of next 10 sc, fpdc around next fpdc, sc in each of next 4 sc, berry st in next sc, sc in next sc, berry st in next sc, sc in each of next 4 sc, fpdc around next fpdc , *sc in each of next 11 sc, fpdc around next fpdc, sc in each of next 4 sc, berry st in next sc, sc in next sc, berry st in next sc, sc in each of next 4 sc, fpdc around next fpdc, rep from * once, join in first st, turn. (72 *sts*)

Rnd 45: Rep rnd 3. (72 *sc*)

Rnd 46: Ch 1, sc in same st as beg ch-1, sc in each of next 4 sc, berry st in next sc, sc in each of next 5 sc, fpdc around next fpdc, *sc in each of next 5 sc, berry st in next sc, sc in each of next 5 sc, fpdc around next fpdc, rep from * 4 times, join in first st, turn. (72 *sts*)

Rnd 47: Rep rnd 3. (72 *sc*)

Rnds 48–62: Rep rnds 24–38.

HOOD
Row 63: Now working in rows, ch 1, sc in each of next 51 sc, leaving rem sts unworked, turn. (51 *sc*)

Row 64: Ch 1, sc in first sc, fpdc around next fpdc, *sc in each of next 11 sc, fpdc around next fpdc, sc in each of next 2 sc, berry st in next sc, sc in each of next 5 sc, berry st in next sc, sc in each of next 2 sc, fpdc around next fpdc, rep from * once, sc in last sc, turn. (51 *sts*)

Row 65: Ch 1, sc in each sc across, turn. (51 *sc*)

Row 66: Ch 1, sc in first sc, fpdc around next fpdc, *sc in each of next 11 sc, fpdc around next fpdc, sc in each of next 3 sc, berry st in next sc, sc in each of next 3 sc, berry st in next sc, sc in each of next 3 sc, fpdc around next fpdc, rep from * once, sc in last sc, turn. (51 *sts*)

Row 67: Rep row 65. (51 *sc*)

Row 68: Ch 1, sc in first sc, fpdc around next fpdc, *sc in each of next 11 sc, fpdc around next fpdc, sc in each of next 4 sc, berry st in next sc, sc in next sc, berry st in next sc, sc in each of next 4 sc, fpdc around next fpdc, rep from * once, sc in last sc, turn. (51 *sts*)

Row 69: Rep row 65. (51 *sc*)

Row 70: Ch 1, sc in first sc, fpdc around next fpdc, *sc in each of next 5 sc, berry st in next sc, sc in each of next 5 sc, fpdc around next fpdc, rep from * 3 times, sc in last sc, turn. (51 *sts*)

Row 71: Rep row 65. (51 *sc*)

Row 72: Ch 1, sc in first sc, fpdc around next fpdc, *sc in each of next 4 sc, berry st in next sc, sc in next sc, berry st in next sc, sc in each of next 4 sc, fpdc around next fpdc, sc in each of next 11 sc, fpdc around next fpdc, rep from * once, sc in last sc, turn (51 *sts*)

Row 73: Rep row 65. (51 *sc*)

Row 74: Ch 1, sc in first sc, fpdc around next fpdc, *sc in each of next 3 sc, berry st in next sc, sc in each of next 3 sc, berry st in next sc, sc in each of next 3 sc, fpdc around next fpdc, sc in each of next 11 sc, fpdc around next fpdc, rep from * once, sc in last sc, turn (51 *sts*)

Row 75: Rep row 65. (51 *sc*)

Row 76: Ch 1, sc in first sc, fpdc around next fpdc, *sc in each of next 2 sc, berry st in next sc, sc in each of next 5 sc, berry st in next sc, sc in each of next 2 sc, fpdc around next fpdc, sc in each of next 11 sc, fpdc around next fpdc, rep from * once, sc in last sc, turn. (51 *sts*)

Note: Remainder of Hood is worked in 3 sections.

LEFT SIDE OF HOOD
Row 77: Ch 1, sc in each of next 15 sts, leaving rem sts unworked, turn. (15 *sc*)

Row 78: Ch 1, sc in first sc, fpdc around next fpdc, sc in each of next 5 sc, berry st in next sc, sc in each of next 5 sc, fpdc around next fpdc, sc in last sc, turn. (15 *sts*)

Row 79: Ch 1, sc in each st across, turn. (15 *sc*)

Row 80: Ch 1, sc in first sc, fpdc around next fpdc, sc in each of next 4 sc, berry st in next sc, sc in next sc, berry st in next sc, sc in each of next 4 sc, fpdc around next fpdc, sc in last sc, turn. (15 *sts*)

Row 81: Rep row 79. (15 *sc*)

Row 82: Ch 1, sc in first sc, fpdc around next fpdc, sc in each of next 3 sc, berry st in next sc, sc in each of next 3 sc, berry st in next sc, sc in each of next 3 sc, fpdc around next fpdc, sc in last sc, turn. *(15 sts)*

Row 83: Rep row 79. *(15 sc)*

Row 84: Ch 1, sc in first sc, fpdc around next fpdc, sc in each of next 2 sc, berry st in next sc, sc in each of next 5 sc, berry st in next sc, sc in each of next 2 sc, fpdc around next fpdc, sc in last sc, turn. *(15 sts)*

Row 85: Rep row 79. *(15 sc)*

Row 86: Ch 1, sc in first sc, fpdc around next fpdc, sc in next sc, berry st in next sc, sc in each of next 3 sc, berry st in next sc, sc in each of next 3 sc, berry st in next sc, sc in next sc, fpdc around next fpdc, sc in last sc, turn. *(15 sts)*

Row 87: Rep row 79. *(15 sc)*

Row 88: Rep row 84. *(15 sts)*

Row 89: Rep row 79. *(15 sc)*

Row 90: Rep row 82. *(15 sts)*

Row 91: Rep row 79. *(15 sc)*

Row 92: Rep row 80. *(15 sts)*

Row 93: Rep row 79. *(15 sc)*

Row 94: Rep row 78. *(15 sts)*

Row 95: Rep row 79. Leaving 12-inch tail, fasten off. *(15 sc)*

MIDDLE SECTION OF HOOD

Row 77: With H hook, join in next sk sc on row 76, ch 1, sc in each of next 22 sts, leaving rem sts unworked, turn. *(22 sc)*

Row 78: Ch 1, sc in each of next 5 sc, berry st in next sc, sc in each of next 5 sc, fpdc around next fpdc, sc in next sc, berry st in next sc, sc in each of next 3 sc, berry st in next sc, sc in each of next 4 sc, turn. *(22 sts)*

Row 79: Ch 1, sc in each st across, turn. *(22 sc)*

Row 80: Ch 1, sc in each of next 4 sc, berry st in next sc, sc in next sc, berry st in next sc, sc in each of next 4 sc, fpdc around next fpdc, sc in each of next 2 sc, berry st in next sc, sc in each of next 5 sc, berry st in next sc, sc in last sc, turn. *(22 sts)*

Row 81: Rep row 79. *(22 sc)*

Row 82: Ch 1, sc in each of next 3 sc, berry st in next sc, sc in each of next 3 sc, berry st in next sc, sc in each of next 3 sc, fpdc around next fpdc, sc in each of next 3 sc, berry st in next sc, sc in each of next 3 sc, berry st in next sc, sc in each of last 2 sc, turn. *(22 sts)*

Row 83: Rep row 79. *(22 sc)*

Row 84: Ch 1, sc in each of next 2 sc, berry st in next sc, sc in each of next 5 sc, berry st in next sc, sc in each of next 2 sc, fpdc around next fpdc, sc in each of next 4 sc, berry st in next sc, sc in next sc, berry st in next sc, sc in each of last 3 sc, turn. *(22 sts)*

Row 85: Rep row 79. *(22 sc)*

Row 86: Ch 1, sc in next sc, berry st in next sc, sc in each of next 3 sc, berry st in next sc, sc in each of next 3 sc, berry st in next sc, sc in next sc, fpdc around next fpdc, sc in each of next 5 sc, berry st in next sc, sc in each of next 4 sc, turn. Leaving 12-inch tail, fasten off. *(22 sts)*

RIGHT SIDE OF HOOD

Row 77: With H hook, join in same sc as last sc on row 76, ch 1, sc in same st as beg ch-1, sc in each of next 14 sc, turn. *(15 sc)*

Row 78: Ch 1, sc in first sc, fpdc around next fpdc, sc in next sc, berry st in next sc, sc in each of next 3 sc, berry st in next sc, sc in each of next 3 sc, berry st in next sc, sc in next sc, fpdc around next fpdc, sc in last sc, turn. *(15 sts)*

Row 79: Ch 1, sc in each st across, turn. *(15 sc)*

Row 80: Ch 1, sc in first sc, fpdc around next fpdc, sc in each of next 2 sc, berry st in next sc,

sc in each of next 5 sc, berry st in next sc, sc in each of next 2 sc, fpdc around next fpdc, sc in last sc, turn. *(15 sts)*

Row 81: Rep row 79. *(15 sc)*

Row 82: Ch 1, sc in first sc, fpdc around next fpdc, sc in each of next 3 sc, berry st in next sc, sc in each of next 3 sc, berry st in next sc, sc in each of next 3 sc, fpdc around next fpdc, sc in last sc, turn. *(15 sts)*

Row 83: Rep row 79. *(15 sc)*

Row 84: Ch 1, sc in first sc, fpdc around next fpdc, sc in each of next 4 sc, berry st in next sc, sc in next sc, berry st in next sc, sc in each of next 4 sc, fpdc around next fpdc, sc in last sc, turn. *(15 sts)*

Row 85: Rep row 79. *(15 sc)*

Row 86: Ch 1, sc in first sc, fpdc around next fpdc, sc in each of next 5 sc, berry st in next sc, sc in each of next 5 sc, fpdc around next fpdc, sc in last sc, turn. *(15 sts)*

Row 87: Rep row 79. *(15 sc)*

Row 88: Ch 1, sc in first sc, fpdc around next fpdc, sc in each of next 11 sc, fpdc around next fpdc, sc in last sc, turn. *(15 sc)*

Row 89: Rep row 79. *(15 sc)*

Rows 90–95: [Rep rows 88 and 89 alternately] 3 times. Leaving 12-inch tail, fasten off at end of row 95.

HOOD ASSEMBLY
Turn Cocoon WS out, holding row 95 from Left Side and Right Side tog, working through both thicknesses, sew or sc sides tog. Bring Middle Section up to meet Left and Right Sides and easing to fit, sew all ends of rows from Middle Section and Left and Right Sides tog, and sew row 95 to top of joined Sides *(see photo).*

FACE OPENING TRIM
Rnd 1: With H hook, join in last st of row 77 of Right Side of Hood, ch 1, working in end of each row and in each st around, sc in each st and in end of each row around, join in first st. *(82 sc)*

Rnd 2: Ch 1, sc in same st as beg ch-1, sc in each of next 3 sc, sk next sc, *sc in each of next 4 sc, sk next sc, rep from * around to last sc, sc in last sc, join in first st. *(65 sc)*

Rnd 3: Ch 1, sc in each sc around, join in first st. Fasten off and weave in ends. *(65 sc)* ∎

Angel
Cocoon Set

FINISHED SIZES
Instructions given fit size newborn–3 months

FINISHED GARMENT MEASUREMENTS
Cocoon: Approx 17½ inches long x
  18 inches circumference
Beanie: Approx 5 inches long x
  12 inches circumference

MATERIALS
- Omega Sol fine (sport) weight yarn (1¾ oz/164 yds/50g per skein):
    8 skeins #1001 white
    2 skeins each #1020 light beige
    and #1022 beige
- Size E/4/3.5mm and size H/8/5mm crochet hooks or size needed to obtain gauge
- Stitch marker

GAUGE
With size H hook: 4 sc = 1 inch; 4 sc rows = 1 inch

PATTERN NOTES
Work in continuous rounds. Do not join or turn unless otherwise stated.

Mark rounds with stitch marker.

Join with slip stitch unless otherwise stated.

Work with 2 strands held together unless otherwise stated.

INSTRUCTIONS
COCOON
Rnd 1: With size H hook and **2 strands of white held tog** *(see Pattern Notes)*, ch 2, 12 sc in 2nd ch from hook. **Do not join** *(see Pattern Notes)*. **Place marker** *(see Pattern Notes)* at end of rnd. *(12 sc)*

Rnd 2: *Sc in next sc, 2 sc in next sc, rep from * around. *(18 sc)*

Rnd 3: *Sc in each of next 2 sc, 2 sc in next sc, rep from * around. *(24 sc)*

Rnd 4: *Sc in each of next 3 sc, 2 sc in next sc, rep from * around. *(30 sc)*

Rnd 5: *Sc in each of next 4 sc, 2 sc in next sc, rep from * around. *(36 sc)*

Rnd 6: *Sc in each of next 5 sc, 2 sc in next sc, rep from * around. *(42 sc)*

Rnd 7: *Sc in each of next 6 sc, 2 sc in next sc, rep from * around. *(48 sc)*

Rnd 8: *Sc in each of next 7 sc, 2 sc in next sc, rep from * around. *(54 sc)*

Rnd 9: *Sc in each of next 8 sc, 2 sc in next sc, rep from * around. *(60 sc)*

Rnd 10: *Sc in each of next 9 sc, 2 sc in next sc, rep from * around. *(66 sc)*

Rnd 11: *Sc in each of next 10 sc, 2 sc in next sc, rep from * around. *(72 sc)*

Rnd 12: Sc in each sc around. *(72 sc)*